Vitality

Written by John Parsons

Contents	Page
Chapter 1. *Vitamin A*	4
Chapter 2. *Vitamin B*	8
Chapter 3. *Vitamin C*	14
Chapter 4. *Vitamin D*	20
Chapter 5. *Vitamin E*	24
Chapter 6. *Vitamin K*	28
Vitamin Reference Chart	31
Index and Bookweb Links	32
Glossary	Inside Back Cover

Rigby

Chapter Snapshots

Imagine if each human body had its own newspaper published daily. What would it report on? What would be the major stories of the day? What would be the major issues that the cells of the body would want to know about?

In this book, we take a look at an imaginary week in the life of a normal human body, aged about 12 years old. The newspaper, called *Vitality Voice*, concentrates on stories about the comings and goings of vitamins in the body — but there's plenty of other news for interested readers. And, like all newspapers, there are also advertisements, weather reports, and letters to the editor! Follow the stories as the top reporters from *Vitality Voice* discover all the news that's happening in a busy body — just like your own!

"All the news fit to eat!"

1. Monday, July 12: Vitamin A   Page 4
2. Tuesday, July 13: Vitamin B   Page 8
3. Wednesday, July 14: Vitamin C   Page 14
4. Thursday, July 15: Vitamin D   Page 20
5. Friday July, 16: Vitamin E   Page 24
6. Saturday, July 17: Vitamin K   Page 28

ISSUE No. 3650

Chapter 1.

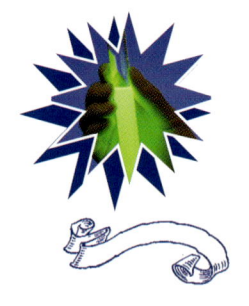

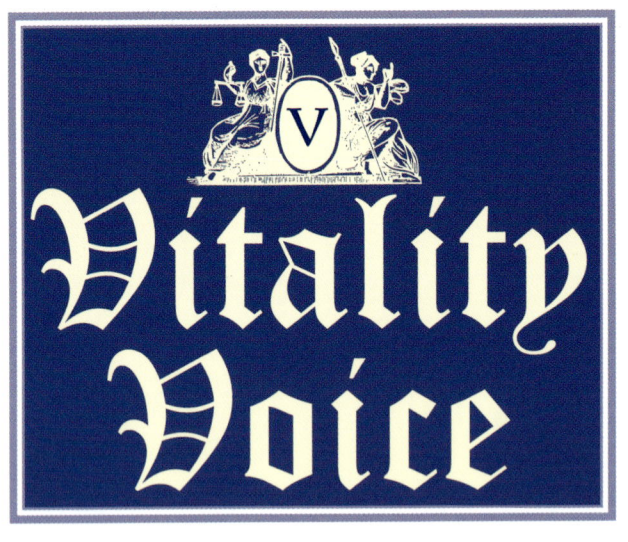

Vitality Voice

Monday
JULY 12

Twelfth Year in Print.

50 cents

The Daily Newspaper That Prints All the News Fit to Eat!

Vitamin A Levels At All-Time High!

EXCLUSIVE REPORT!

Following a large meal of carrots, sweet potato, and pumpkin, eaten in the form of a fresh vegetable soup last night, vitamin A levels are reported to be at an all-time high level today.

Vitamin A is essential for vision and the eyes. It also gives the body healthy skin, bones, and helps it to fight against infections.

4

Read All About It in Today's Issue!

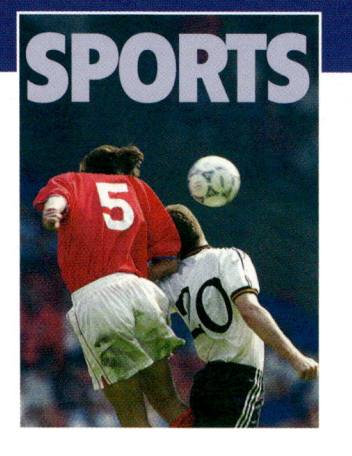

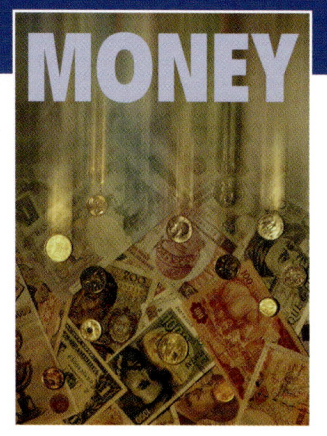

TV — **SPORTS** — **MONEY**

Vitamin Danger, Warning Issued!

As vitamin A is one of the few vitamins that can be poisonous if too much is eaten, the body is warned against eating large amounts of any foods containing vitamin A for the next few days.

The best source of vitamin A is liver, but as the body belongs to a twelve-year-old child, there is little danger of too much of that being eaten. Vitamin A can also be found in yellow fruits, such as paw paw, mangoes, and rock melons.

Weather Outlook

A warm 98·6°F, with cooler temperatures in the morning around the feet and fingers. A hot shower is expected late in the evening, when temperatures will rise briefly.

5

Vitality Voice, Monday, July 12

A Fatty Meal is Eaten

Reports have been received of a grilled sandwich being recently consumed by the body. The grilled sandwich appears to have been prepared using butter and cheese, both of which contain polyunsaturated fats.

"Be on the lookout," warns immune system spokesperson.

A spokesperson for the body's immune system has released a statement warning all cells to be on the lookout for free radicals. The spokesperson's statement explains that free radicals are produced when polyunsaturated fats break down inside the body. Free radicals can cause wrinkly skin and cell damage. If any free radicals are spotted, they should be avoided. The statement advises that antioxidants, such as vitamin C, will help to destroy the free radicals.

Fresh milk is healthy to drink — but when it's made into butter, we say "take it easy!"

Cows' Comment!

Vitality Voice, Monday, July 12

Vitality Voice Classified Ads

To place your ad, call our Classified hot line on 1-800-ADSFORU. $1.50 per line.

Employment

Attention: Vitamin C molecules urgently needed by the circulatory system to fight common cold viruses. Plenty of work available for vitamin C molecules who wish to play an important part in keeping the body free of sneezes and sniffles over the coming week. Call 987-6543 or e-mail vitaminc@veins.bod.

Public Notice

All vitamins, minerals, cells, and other body parts are advised that this body will shut down for minor repairs between 9:00 P.M. and 7:00 A.M. A healthy breakfast of cereal, milk, and fruit juice at 7:30 A.M. will boost vitamin levels after the repairs are complete.

Funky!

Where does the word *vitamin* come from? It was invented in 1912 by a Polish biochemist named Casimir Funk. At first, people thought there were only two vitamins, one that dissolved in water and one that dissolved in fat.

Two American scientists discovered that these vitamins were actually mixtures. Since then, 13 vitamins have been found. The last was vitamin B12 in 1948.

Vitamin Vision

A biochemist named George Wald discovered that the body makes a chemical called *retinene* from vitamin A. Retinene reacts with light at the back of the eye and enables us to see.

In 1967, Wald was awarded the Nobel Prize for Medicine for his discovery.

ISSUE No. 3651

Chapter 2.

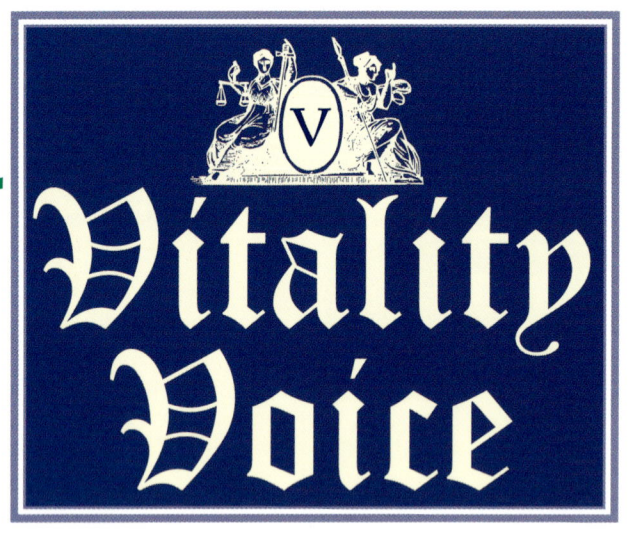

Vitality Voice

Tuesday
JULY 13

Twelfth Year in Print.

50 cents

The Daily Newspaper That Prints All the News Fit to Eat!

Vitamin B Family Members Celebrate!

Shock Disappearance of Vitamins: Report, Page 10

Large celebrations are expected today as members of the B family of vitamins hold their annual reunion.

As one of the most numerous vitamin families, with a total of eight different members, vitamins in the B family have found it necessary to sometimes use numbers to tell each other apart. Other members of the vitamin B family prefer to be known by their scientific names. For a complete listing of vitamin B family members, see page 9.

8

Free Today! Exclusive Vitamin B Guide!

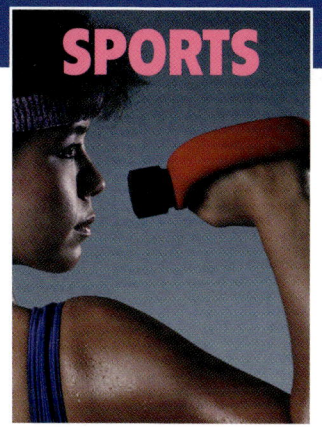

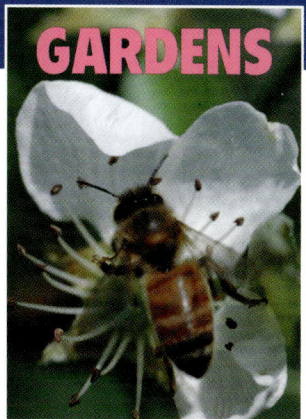

TRAVEL **SPORTS** **GARDENS**

To B Or Not To B: Exclusive Guide

Need to know who's a *B* and who's not? Use your exclusive Vitamin B Guide (below) for a complete list of the vitamin B family members, and where they are likely to be found:

Vitamin B1
Cornflakes, yeast extracts, broad beans, brown rice

Vitamin B2
Kidneys, yeast extracts, cornflakes, milk

Vitamin B6
Chicken, fish, meat

Vitamin B12
Liver, kidneys, oysters, fish, avocado, broccoli

Biotin
Egg yolk, peas, soybeans

Niacin
Canned fish, chicken, meat, peanuts

Folic Acid
Asparagus, broccoli, lettuce, spinach

Pantothenic Acid
Meat, eggs

Vitality Voice, Tuesday, July 13

SHOCK B VITAMIN DISAPPEARANCE!

Hot News!

VITAMINS B7–B11 STILL MISSING!

People who are worried about the disappearance of vitamins B3 and B4 should no longer worry, says a vitamin researcher. They are still used in the body, but they are now called niacin.

The whereabouts of vitamin B5 has also been discovered. Vitamin B5 is now happily using the name folic acid. Just what happened to vitamins B7–B11 is still unknown, however. The researcher says it is unlikely that they exist, but that people had to leave space for them just in case!

Vitamin research reveals vitamins B3, B4, and B5 changed their names.

Vitality Voice, Tuesday, July 13

Cholesterol: Good & Bad

Cholesterol molecules circulating in the blood have pointed out that there are actually two types of cholesterol — good and bad. They hope to remind all cells, particularly those in blood vessels, that cholesterol is needed by every cell to make healthy walls.

> "We just want to be left alone …" says cholesterol molecule.

"Every body manufactures its own good cholesterol," said one cholesterol molecule. "I was made in the liver, like millions of others."

"It's when there is too much of the bad cholesterol eaten, in animal fats, that we lose balance." Too much cholesterol can cause a build-up of fat inside blood vessels and may cause blockages. "We just want to be left alone to do our job. The liver can make all the good cholesterol needed — so why would anyone want to eat too many animal fats, such as butter, cream, fatty meats, shrimp, or eggs? It just doesn't make sense!" said one concerned cholesterol molecule.

Classifieds, Now on Page 12

Vitality Voice, Tuesday, July 13

Vitality Voice Classified Ads
To place your ad, call our Classified hot line on 1-800-ADSFORU. $1.50 per line.

Public Notice

Due to secretly watching TV way past bedtime, last night's sleep hours were insufficient to allow all the body's repairs to be carried out. An extra hour of sleep has been allocated for this morning. Don't wake the body up!

Weather Outlook

A warm 98.6°F, dropping down to 97.7°F when the body dives into a cold swimming pool. Normal temperatures will resume after some shivering.

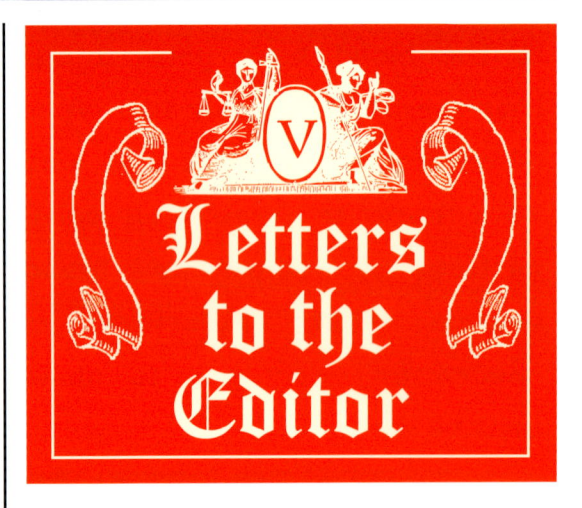

Letters to the Editor

Dear Editor,

Why are vitamins always in the limelight? It's time people realized that minerals are essential too!

An Unappreciated Mineral

(See our special feature, p.13. Editor)

Nice, but no Niacin

When the Spanish introduced corn into Europe from America, in the early 1700s, many people began to use it as their main source of food. It seemed healthy and filling. What they didn't know was that corn has no niacin in it. Soon, a disease caused by niacin deficiency, called pellagra, spread across Europe. Corn alone was not a balanced diet.

Vitality Voice, Tuesday, July 13

Essential Minerals

As well as vitamins, the body needs a variety of minerals to grow and stay healthy. As minerals cannot be manufactured by the body, they need to be taken into the body as part of a healthy diet.

Minerals are used in almost every cell and part of the body. They help the body to perform the chemical reactions it needs to convert food into energy and to carry gases such as oxygen around in the blood. Minerals, such as calcium, also make up a large part of the body, in the form of bones and teeth. The following minerals are the major minerals that the body needs every day.

Minerals:	Chemical Signs:
Calcium	Ca
Chlorine	Cl
Magnesium	Mg
Phosphorus	P
Potassium	K
Sodium	Na
Sulfur	S

Trace Elements

The body needs other minerals in much smaller quantities. These minerals are called trace elements. They include chromium, copper, fluorine, iodine, iron, manganese, molybdenum, selenium and zinc.

ISSUE No. 3652

Chapter 3.

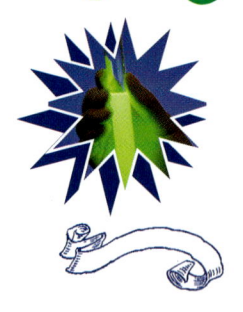

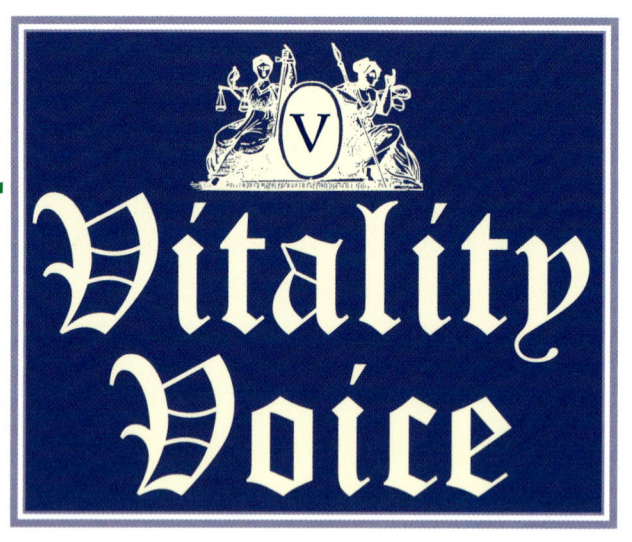

Vitality Voice

Wednesday
JULY 14

Twelfth Year in Print.

50 cents

The Daily Newspaper That Prints All the News Fit to Eat!

IS THIS THE WORLD'S FAVORITE VITAMIN?

See our EXCLUSIVE report, page 15!

Plus Inside This Issue:
Movie Reviews: Section B
Latest Sports: Section C
Today's Weather: Section D

14

VITAMIN C VOTED MOST POPULAR VITAMIN!

By Sue Scurvilla, Health Reporter

Up to 20% of the population regularly takes extra vitamin C to ward off colds, coughs, and sneezes, reports Sue Scurvilla, our health reporter.

Amazingly, most people are already getting plenty of vitamin C through their regular diet. It is by far the most well-known and popular vitamin, and its benefits have been studied for many years.

Before vitamin C was discovered, many sailors and travelers who could not eat fresh fruit and vegetables became sick due to lack of vitamin C. This sickness is called scurvy and did cause some people on long journeys to die.

More EXCLUSIVE Vitamin C Health News: SEE PAGE 16!

Sources of vitamin C include lemons (1), oranges (2), strawberries (3), other citrus fruits (4), and kiwifruit (5).

Vitality Voice, Wednesday, July 14

TOP SOURCES OF VITAMIN C REVEALED!

"The announcement . . . came as a surprise to many people."

By Citronella Tart, Investigative Reporter

Red peppers, guavas, and brussels sprouts are the winners in the recent competition to find the top sources of vitamin C.

Runners-up include oranges, lemons, and limes, and other fresh fruit such as kiwifruit, cranberries, strawberries, and grapefruit.

The announcement of red peppers as the number one source of vitamin C came as a surprise to many people. Most people didn't realize that if they ate only half a cup of red peppers each day, they would be eating over three times the amount of vitamin C they need!

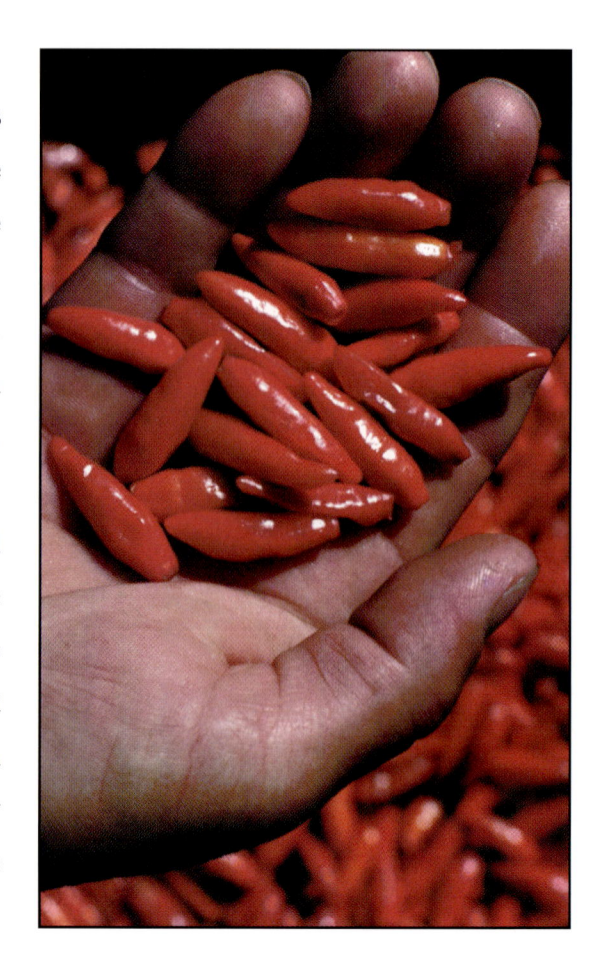

Vitality Voice, Wednesday, July 14

FALSE VITAMIN ALERT!

Weather Outlook

A warm 98·6°F, cooler in the afternoon due to getting wet in a rain shower. A period of running quickly back to the house is expected to raise the body temperature back to normal again shortly afterwards.

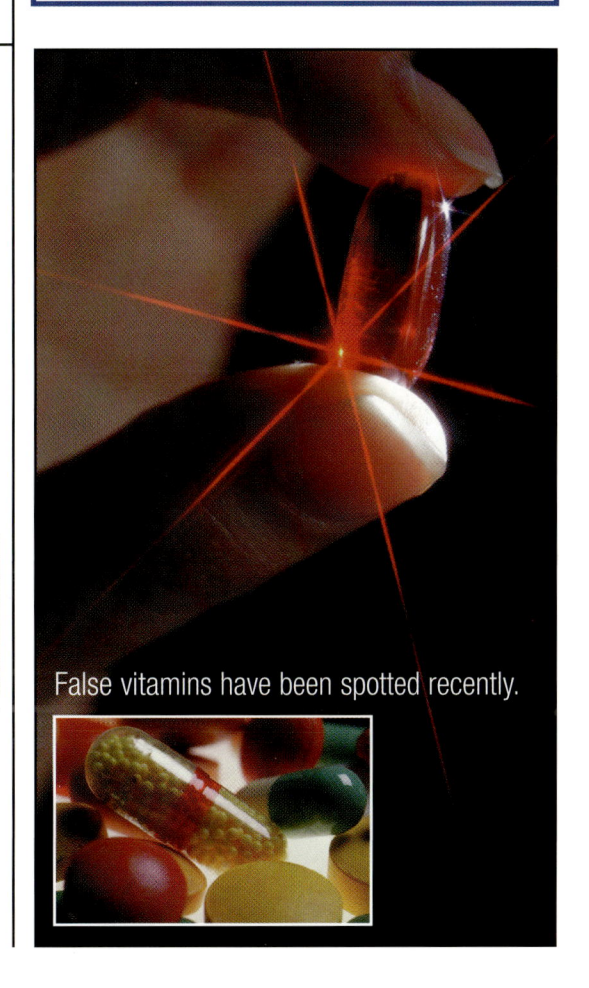

A few false vitamins have been spotted recently, and people are warned that they should not be fooled into buying expensive vitamin pills that claim to contain extra vitamins.

The main culprits have been two chemicals claiming to be called vitamin B15 and B17.

"No evidence"

Studies show that neither of these so-called B vitamins are actually vitamins, and there is no evidence that they are of any benefit to people's bodies.

False vitamins have been spotted recently.

17

Vitality Voice, Wednesday, July 14

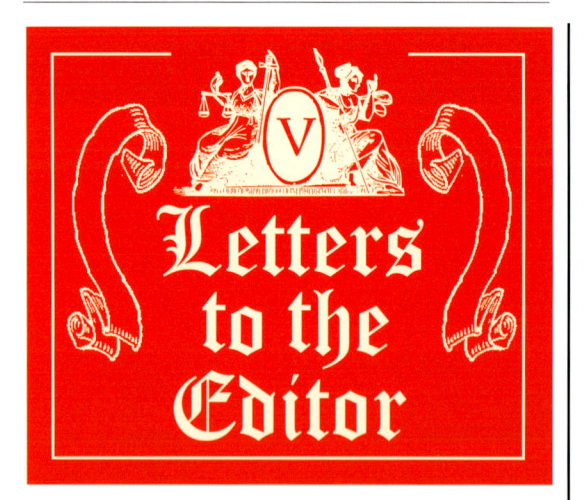

Letters to the Editor

Dear Editor,

I wish to express my concern that some members of the vitamin B group, namely biotins, are trying to have their own vitamin group named after them. Several biotins have been going around using the name vitamin H, which seems silly. If they are the same thing, why confuse people with different names? And anyway, I can't see the point of choosing a letter like H. If vitamins are going to set up their own group, they should choose the next letter that hasn't already been taken. What's wrong with F or G?

Sincerely yours,
A Concerned Chemical

VITAMINS REQUEST LESS COOKING

By Caramel Chew, Cooking Reporter

"Don't overcook us," say a group of concerned vitamins who are easily destroyed by too much heat.

The group, which includes vitamins B, C, and E, say that some people are cooking foods for too long. This cooking destroys as much as 70% of all their vitamin members in a food. The group says that while some foods, such as meat, eggs, and fish, obviously need to be well cooked, others, such as vegetables and fruit, taste just as good when they are eaten raw.

"All people need to do is cook us less or eat us raw," said one spokesperson for the group.

18

Vitality Voice, Wednesday, July 14

Vitality Voice Classified Ads

To place your ad, call our Classified hot line on 1-800-ADSFORU. $1.50 per line.

Employment

Positions are available for iron molecules, currently required to help red blood cells carry oxygen around the body. Colorful uniform provided. Please apply to Bone Marrow, Skeleton.

Public Notice

Due to an unforeseen lack of fruit for breakfast, all cells are advised that vitamin C levels will be low for the first half of the day. Further supplies are expected to be received around lunchtime.

Lost & Found

Lost, due to lack of vitamins: CONCENTRATION! Please return!

Limeys

Scurvy is a fatal disease caused by a lack of vitamin C. Hundreds of years ago, sailors on long sea journeys ate few fresh foods, and many died of scurvy. In 1795, the British navy started giving lime juice to their sailors. Suddenly, the incidence of scurvy dropped. Since then, a common nickname for British sailors has been 'limeys.'

Cobalt

Vitamin B12 contains cobalt, a mineral found in the soil. Some soils have no cobalt, however. Cobalt is added to animal feed to ensure farm animals get enough vitamin B12.

ISSUE No. 3653

Chapter 4.

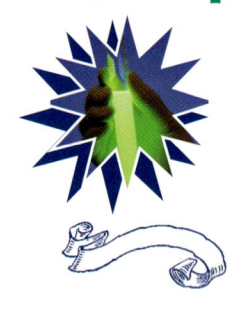

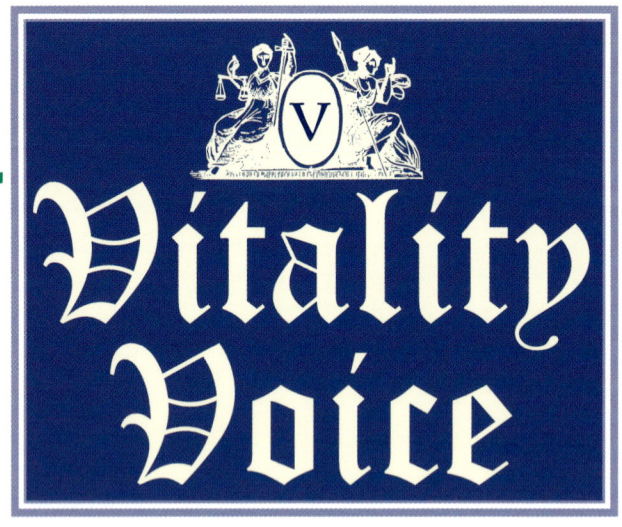

Vitality Voice

Thursday
JULY 15
Twelfth Year in Print.

50 cents

The Daily Newspaper That Prints All the News Fit to Eat!

SUNNY DAYS!

EXCELLENT NEWS FOR VITAMIN D LEVELS

By Sam Solario, Weather Reporter

The recent bright sunny weather has been excellent news for levels of vitamin D.

This is one of the few vitamins that does not occur at all in fruit or vegetables. Instead, it is made by the body when sunlight shines on the skin.

People who lived in smoggy or polluted cities in the past, and who did not get enough sunshine,

Report continues, page 21

Sunny Days, continued from page 20

sometimes suffered from a lack of vitamin D. Poor bones and teeth can sometimes result from a lack of vitamin D.

In far northern countries, like Russia, where there is often no sunshine for many months of the year, many children in schools use artificial sunlamps to keep healthy.

Ultraviolet Rays

While ultraviolet, or UV, rays are important for making vitamin D, too much exposure may lead to sunburn or skin cancer. Hats, clothing, sunglasses, and sunscreen should always be worn for protection from UV rays when exposure to the sun is expected.

VITAMIN D SUCCESSFULLY STORED!

Unlike many vitamins, vitamin D can be successfully stored by the body. This is helpful for short periods when there is little sunshine.

Studies have revealed that vitamin D passes slowly from the skin into the body, where it is stored in muscle and fat. Even though vitamin D can be stored, health authorities say that people should still try to get out into natural light regularly for short periods.

Vitality Voice, Thursday, July 15

Letters to the Editor

Weather Outlook

A warm 98·6°F, rising to 100.4°F due to the effects of a flu virus that was discovered yesterday. Body temperatures are expected to remain slightly higher than normal for a day or two.

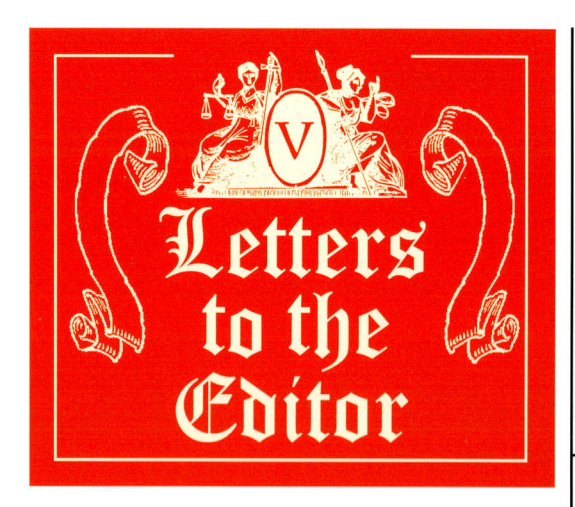

Dear Editor,

After reading yesterday's letter from "A Concerned Chemical," I would like to point out that biotins are not the only ones who have sometimes used letters to look like their own vitamin group. Perhaps the finger should be pointed at folic acids. In the past, folic acid tried to set up their own vitamin group, called vitamin M! One can only wonder what happened to all the earlier letters. Perhaps they were not good enough?

Sincerely yours,
A Bothered Biotin

CALCIUM NAMED AS MOST COMMON MINERAL

Calcium has won the title of "Most Common Mineral" in the body. About 99% of all calcium in the body is found in the bones. In second place was magnesium. About 65% of all magnesium is found in the bones, too. It appears that, for popular minerals, the skeleton is the place to be!

Vitality Voice, Thursday, July 15

Vitality Voice Classified Ads
To place your ad, call our Classified hot line on 1-800-ADSFORU. $1.50 per line.

For Sale

Old clear glass milk bottles. As vitamin B2, contained in milk, is easily destroyed by light, all milk is now packaged in cardboard cartons or colored plastic bottles.

Public Notice

A haircut will occur at 5:00 P.M. this afternoon. Any vitamin E volunteers, willing to help regrow shiny new hair, required urgently.

Wanted

Supply of vitamin B12 required by vegetarian. As no vegetables or fruits contain any vitamin B12, supplements of this vitamin may be required by vegetarian who eats no animal or dairy products.

Subscribe to Vitality Voice now, and receive a 10% discount off the cover price! Only 45 cents!

PUBLIC SERVICE ANNOUNCEMENT

Recent sunny days have raised concerns by small amounts of vitamin A that they may be in danger.

Vitamin A is destroyed by too much sunlight, so people are advised to store milk and other sources of vitamin A in dark places. Correct packaging in bottles and cartons that do not let light through can also help.

ISSUE No. 3654

Chapter 5.

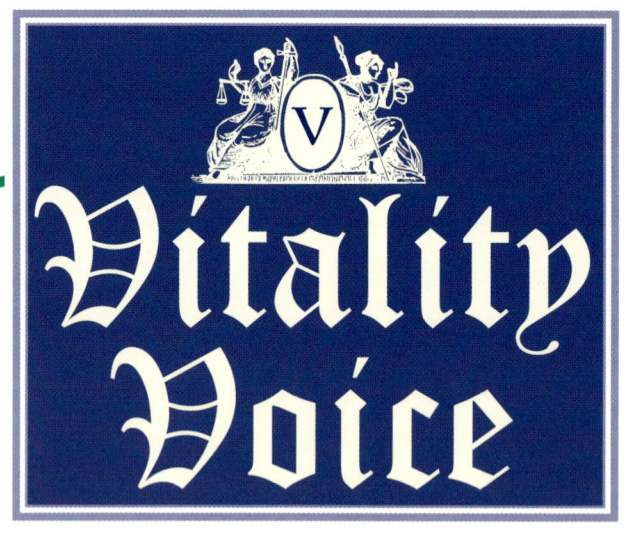

Vitality Voice

Friday
JULY 16
Twelfth Year in Print.

50 cents

The Daily Newspaper That Prints All the News Fit to Eat!

MYSTERY VITAMIN!

E LINKED TO FATS AND OILS

Whole Wheat Flour Is Best: See page 25

By Olive Grove, Investigative Reporter

Mystery still surrounds the actual use of vitamin E. Many people believe that it is essential for children's good health, but studies have yet to prove or disprove this.

It seems likely that vitamin E is used to make healthy red blood cells and to keep the skins of cells strong. One of the major sources of vitamin E appears to be fats and oils, but people are warned against using too much of these substances in their cooking. Heating fats and oils for cooking destroys almost all of the vitamin E in them anyway, so there appears to be no benefit in deep-frying foods in fats and oils.

24

WHOLE WHEAT FLOUR IS BEST!

Another good source of vitamin E is flour — but people are advised that almost all of the vitamin E is contained in the outer husk, or brown part of the wheat seed.

When the husk is removed to produce white flour, very little vitamin E remains. Researchers recommend that whole wheat flour be used wherever possible.

Special Feature
GREAT MISTAKES OF THE PAST

This new report looks at some silly mistakes made in the past. While lemons and limes were known to be good sources of vitamin C, they were difficult to store on ships.

"Lemons and limes..."

To give sailors enough vitamins, new ways of storing these fruits were invented. One of them was to make a drink by boiling the juice of lemons and limes until it was thick and syrupy. Unfortunately, boiling destroyed almost all of the vitamin C in the juice. Sailors who drank the syrup became just as sick as those who didn't have any lemon or lime juice!

Vitality Voice, Friday, July 16

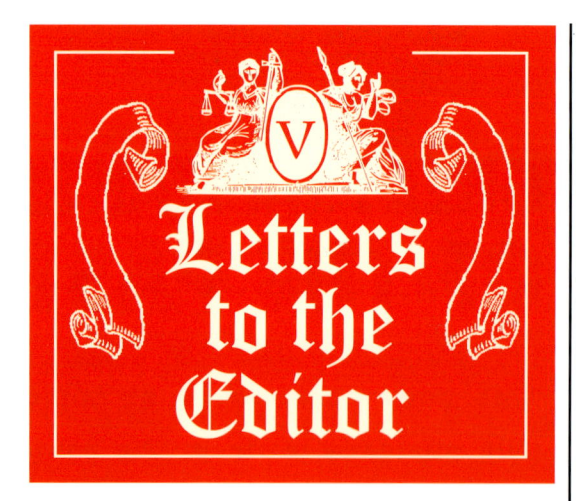

Letters to the Editor

Dear Editor,

I would like to express my thanks to our friend, vitamin E, for its role in helping to store vitamin A molecules in the body.

As everyone knows, we can sometimes be broken down by other chemicals attacking us in the blood. This can result in low vitamin A levels. The action of vitamin E in helping to slow down the attacks means that we are kept at healthy levels. Thank you, and best wishes.

Sincerely yours,
Vitamin A

Restless Legs!

Lack of vitamin E can cause "restless leg syndrome," causing tossing and turning at night. It was first described in a medical book from 1685:

"In arms and legs, leapings and contractions of the tendons, and so great a restlessness and tossing of their limbs ensue, that the diseased are no more able to sleep than if they were in a place of the greatest torture!"

Weather Outlook

A hot 99·5°F, resulting from the body's fight against the flu virus. Some discomfort will be felt throughout the night, but the temperature is expected to return to normal tomorrow afternoon.

Vitality Voice, Friday, July 16

Vitality Voice Classified Ads

To place your ad, call our Classified hot line on 1-800-ADSFORU. $1.50 per line.

Wanted

Spare calcium molecules wanted by arm bone, recently broken in cycling accident. Please call by the ulna bone, just below the elbow, at your earliest opportunity.

Public Notices

Salty snacks will be eaten before dinner-time tonight. All cells are advised that an overdose of sodium chloride (or salt) is expected for a couple of hours after eating the snacks. Cells are urged to retain as much water as possible to avoid being harmed.

Brain cells are requested to make the body feel thirsty as soon as possible to correct the imbalance quickly.

Dangers Of Technology

Since vitamins were first discovered in the early 1900s, people have been using technology to create synthetic, or artificial, vitamins to use when the diet does not provide enough natural vitamins. Technology also allows us to manufacture pure forms of essential minerals, too.

Some forms of technology may introduce harmful minerals into our environment and our bodies, however. Lead, mercury, and cadmium are dangerous minerals that, for much of the 20th century, were used in many ways. Lead was used in gasoline and paint, mercury was used in mining and chemical manufacture, and cadmium was used in metalwork and paper manufacturing. All can cause severe illness.

ISSUE No. 3655

Chapter 6.

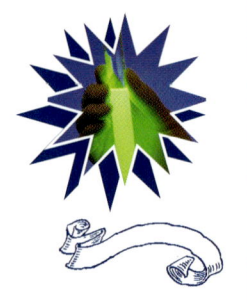

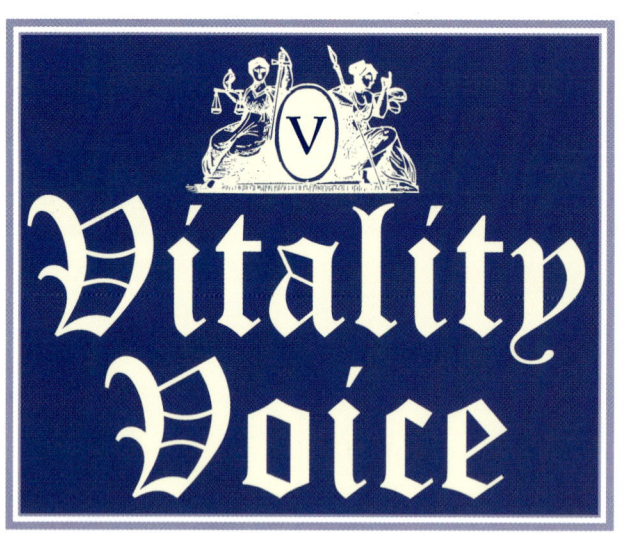

Vitality Voice

Saturday
JULY 17
Twelfth Year in Print.

50 cents

The Daily Newspaper That Prints All the News Fit to Eat!

Vitamin K Hero!

Bleeding from a small scratch received while playing sports has been successfully stopped by the quick action of vitamin K. Vitamin K is essential to help the blood form clots. These clots stop the continued loss of blood from scratches and cuts.

Reports from the site of the injury indicate that, because plenty of fresh vegetables, including

VITAMIN K STOPS BLEEDING
Report continues, page 29

28

Continued from page 28: Vitamin K Stops Bleeding

broccoli, brussels sprouts, lettuce, and spinach, have been eaten in the last few days, there was plenty of vitamin K available to help the blood cells clot. The healthy amounts of vitamin K will also mean that there will be less bruising around the injured area, too.

Almost all fresh vegetables, lightly cooked, contain vitamin K.

"DON'T FORGET US!" SAY BACTERIA

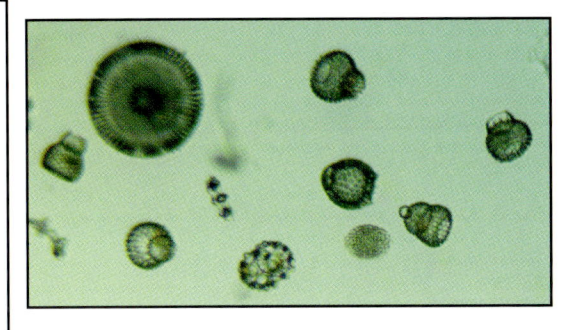

Bacteria in the digestive system are also claiming an important part in the production of vitamin K. "While food is one source of vitamin K, much of the body's requirements are also produced by us," says one bacteria. "Most people are unaware of the fact that many newborn babies have very low amounts of vitamin K in their bodies."

"It's only after babies start eating food which contains helpful bacteria that their vitamin K levels start to grow."

Vitality Voice, Saturday, July 17

Vitality Voice Classified Ads

To place your ad, call our Classified hot line on 1-800-ADSFORU. $1.50 per line.

Wanted

Good storage jars. Vitamin B1 requires good storage jars to prevent attacks by oxygen in the air. Oxygen can easily destroy large amounts of vitamin B1, so proper storage of foods in sealed containers is necessary.

Employment

Clean, strong fluoride molecules required by teeth under attack by tooth decay. Must be willing to work long hours in difficult conditions. Please apply to Molars, 48 Bottom Jaw, Mouth.

Public Notices

All vitamins, minerals, cells, and other body parts are reminded that they must immediately notify the immune system of any unusual bacteria found floating in the blood. Penalties for ignoring unusual bacteria are severe and will be strictly enforced.

Weather Outlook

A warm 98·6°F, warmer in the morning due to a long hot bath.

Odd Ones Out!

Curiously, all plants, fish, insects, and animals — except for three — can manufacture their own vitamin C. Humans, monkeys, and guinea pigs are the odd ones out!

Vitamin Reference Chart

Vitamin	Source	Use
A	Liver, yellow and orange fruits and vegetables	Growth of babies, healthy skin, eyes, bones, and teeth
B1	Cornflakes, yeast, beans, brown rice	Growth, helps change foods into energy
B2	Kidneys, yeast, cornflakes, milk	Growth, helps keep skin and eyes healthy
B6	Chicken, fish, meat	Helps the body make proteins to build cells and muscles
B12	Liver, kidneys, oysters, fish, avocado, broccoli	Helps produce DNA for healthy cells and reproduction
Biotin	Egg yolks, peas, soybeans	Helps the body change fats into energy
Niacin	Canned fish, chicken, meat, peanuts	Helps grow healthy cells and converts food into energy
Folic acid	Asparagus, broccoli, lettuce, spinach	Helps produce DNA for reproduction
Pantothenic Acid	Meat, eggs	Helps produce energy from food
C	Red peppers, citrus fruits, kiwifruit, strawberries	Helps produce healthy blood vessels, bones, and teeth
D	Sunlight	Essential for strong bone growth
E	Vegetable oils, whole wheat flour and grains	Essential for building strong cell walls
K	Broccoli, brussels sprouts, lettuce, spinach	Essential for blood clotting

Index

antioxidants 6
biotin 9, 18, 22
bones 4, 21
butter 6, 11
calcium 22
cheese 6
cholesterol 11
circulatory system 7
cobalt 19
cooking 18
digestive system 29
fats 6, 11, 24
flour 25
folic acid 9, 22
free radicals 6
Funk, Casimir 7
immune system 6
infection 4
lime juice 19, 25
liver 5, 11
magnesium 22
minerals 13, 27
niacin 9, 12
oils 24
pantothenic acid 9
scurvy 15, 19
skin 4, 6
trace elements 13
ultraviolet rays 21
vision 4
vitamin A 4, 5, 7, 23, 26
vitamin B 7–10, 17–19, 23
vitamin C 6, 7, 15, 16, 18, 25, 30
vitamin D 20, 21
vitamin E 6, 18, 23–26
vitamin K 28, 29
Wald, George 7

Bookweb Links

More Bookweb books about nutrition and healthy foods:

Autumn Moon — Fiction
Vote For Us! — Nonfiction
A Chef's Laboratory — Nonfiction

And here's a Bookweb book about how the food chain works in the African grasslands:

Uncool! — Fiction

Key to Bookweb Fact Boxes
☐ Arts
☐ Health
☐ Science
☐ Social Studies
☐ Technology

32